P9-DYE-102

For
Property of
Army Community Service
Fort McPherson, GA

Property of Volunteer Center

LiGHT OnE CaNDLe

Quotes For Hope And Action

Compiled by
Arrington Chambliss
Wayne Meisel
Maura Wolf

Design by
Hobbamock

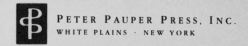
PETER PAUPER PRESS, INC.
WHITE PLAINS · NEW YORK

This book is dedicated to Greg Ricks and Julia Scatliff.

Copyright © 1991
Campus Outreach Opportunity League, Inc.
1511 K Street, N.W., Suite 307
Washington, D.C. 20005
(202) 637-7004

Published by:
Peter Pauper Press, Inc.
202 Mamaroneck Avenue
White Plains, New York 10601
Printed in China
7

Introduction

Each person has heard a call—from a family member, a friend in need, from a homeless person whose eyes met yours on the street, from a leader whose words or deeds inspired you. It wasn't the cause or the issue that touched you, but a human being who reached out and inspired you to serve someone, to do the good work before you.

Across the country, more people are taking time out of their busy lives to do this service and meet community needs. They are tutoring, helping in our nation's troubled schools, working with people with AIDS, developing recycling and other environmental programs. Some may find it surprising, but this is especially true among young people. Challenged by growing social needs and better organized opportunities for community involvement, students are doing service in greater numbers than at any time since the late 1960's.

Working with COOL (Campus Outreach Opportunity League), a national non-profit organization that promotes community service on more than 600 college campuses, we have seen a student community service movement blossom. It's a movement grounded in the spirit of cooperation and inclusiveness, a movement that believes community involvement can be a common ground for all people. It is this movement that has inspired us to compile this collection of words and thoughts and produce this book.

Light One Candle may be a practical resource or source of inspiration. It is organized into five chapters: Challenge, Exploration, Action, Reflection, and Celebration. *Light One Candle* may help you write a speech, a paper, or a sermon. Or it may encourage you to reflect on relationships with others, to work for social justice, to support an issue that concerns you.

In bringing these quotations together, we hope to sound a call, to move the reluctant to action, to sustain others already making a contribution. Eleanor Roosevelt told us, *It's better to light a single candle than to curse the darkness.* You are that candle, and we hope this book helps to kindle and spread the flame, the passion for service, within you.

Arrington Chambliss
Wayne Meisel
Maura Wolf

P.S. The problem of sexism in quotations troubled us throughout. We have attempted to find as many gender neutral quotes as possible, but have not altered or excluded quotes that sound sexist in their original wording.

A Call to Action

If you want to be an activist, you must speak up. For many of us, that step can be the hardest part. We worry that we will be misunderstood, misquoted or, worst of all, tongue-tied. This book will help you develop your own voice through the inspiration and power of other people.

Campus Outreach Opportunity League benefits from the sale of this book. COOL is a national non-profit organization which challenges college students across the country to make a difference through community service. By speaking out and working on such issues as literacy, housing, and the environment, COOL provides a platform for many different voices. These students turn their words into action. They help change our society for the good through their dreams and energy.

The time is now for you to take a stake in this dream too. Buy this book. You'll find eloquence and hope from these pages. COOL and this world depend on you.

Julia Scatliff,
Former Executive Director of COOL

For more information about the Campus Outreach Opportunity League (COOL) write: 1511 K Street, N.W., Suite 307, Washington, D.C. 20005, or call (202) 637-7004.

CHALLENGE

I have a dream...

— Martin Luther King, Jr.

Challenge

I have a dream . . .
Martin Luther King, Jr.

Never doubt that a small group of
thoughtful, committed citizens can change
the world; indeed, it's the only thing that
ever has.

MARGARET MEAD

Love cannot remain by itself—it has no
meaning. Love has to be put into action and
that action is service.

MOTHER TERESA

This country will not be a good place for
any of us to live in unless we make it a good
place for all of us to live in.

THEODORE ROOSEVELT

All humanity is one undivided and indivisible family, and each one of us is responsible for the misdeeds of all the others.

GANDHI

The hottest places in Hell are reserved for those who in time of great moral crises maintain their neutrality.

DANTE

It is better to die on your feet than to live on your knees.

DOLORES IBARRURI
(LA PASIONARA)

I was taught that the world had a lot of problems; that I could struggle and change them; that intellectual and material gifts brought the privilege and responsibility of sharing with others less fortunate; and that service is the rent each of us pays for living—the very purpose of life and not something you do in your spare time or after you have reached your personal goals.

MARIAN WRIGHT EDELMAN

Each time a man stands up for an ideal, or acts to improve the lots of others, or strikes out against injustice, he sends forth a tiny ripple of hope, and crossing each other from a million different centers of energy and daring those ripples build a current which can sweep down the mightiest walls of oppression and resistance.

ROBERT F. KENNEDY

The only thing necessary for evil to triumph is for good men to do nothing.

EDMUND BURKE

"There's no use in trying," she said: "one *can't* believe impossible things." "I daresay you haven't had much practice," said the Queen. "When I was your age, I always did it for half-an-hour a day. Why, sometimes I've believed as many as six impossible things before breakfast."

LEWIS CARROLL

We cannot live for ourselves alone.

VERNON E. JORDAN, JR.

Give me your tired, your poor,
Your huddled masses yearning to breathe
    free,
The wretched refuse of your teeming shore,
Send these, the homeless, tempest-tossed,
    to me:
I lift my lamp beside the golden door.

EMMA LAZARUS,
Inscription for Statue of Liberty

In the end more than they wanted freedom,
they wanted security. When the Athenians
finally wanted not to give to society but for
society to give to them, when the freedom
they wished for was freedom from
responsibility, then Athens ceased to
be free.

EDWARD GIBBON

We must accept finite disappointment, but
we must never lose infinite hope.

MARTIN LUTHER KING, JR.

The greatest challenge of the day is: how to
bring about a revolution of the heart, a
revolution which has to start with each one
of us?

DOROTHY DAY

You cannot hope to build a better world without improving the individuals. To that end each of us must work for his own improvement, and at the same time share a general responsibility for all humanity, our particular duty being to aid those to whom we think we can be most useful.

MARIE CURIE

The ultimate measure of a man is not where he stands in the moments of comfort and convenience, but where he stands in times of challenge and controversy.

MARTIN LUTHER KING, JR.

Many people fear nothing more terribly than to take a position which stands out sharply and clearly from the prevailing opinion. The tendency of most is to adopt a view that is so ambiguous that it will include everything and so popular that it will include everybody. Not a few men who cherish lofty and noble ideals hide them under a bushel for fear of being called different.

MARTIN LUTHER KING, JR.

The dogmas of the quiet past are inadequate to the stormy present. The occasion is piled high with difficulty, and we must rise with the occasion. As our case is new, so we must think anew and act anew. We must disenthrall ourselves, and then we shall save our country.

ABRAHAM LINCOLN

You gain strength, courage and confidence by every experience in which you really stop to look fear in the face . . . You must do the thing you think you cannot do.

ELEANOR ROOSEVELT

Democracy cannot be saved by superman, but only by the unswerving devotion and goodness of millions of little men.

ADLAI E. STEVENSON

Never before have we had so little time in which to do so much.

FRANKLIN DELANO ROOSEVELT

Most Americans have never seen the ignorance, degradation, hunger, sickness, and futility in which many other Americans live . . . They won't become involved in economic or political change until something brings the seriousness of the situation home to them.

SHIRLEY CHISHOLM

The very development of American society is creating a new kind of blindness to poverty. The poor are increasingly slipping out of the very experience and consciousness of the nation.

MICHAEL HARRINGTON

As soon as any man says of the affairs of the State, *What does it matter to me?* the State may be given up for lost.

JEAN JACQUES ROUSSEAU

No man has a right to lead such a life of contemplation as to forget in his own ease the service due to his neighbor.

AUGUSTINE

15

If a free society cannot help the many who are poor, it cannot save the few who are rich.

JOHN F. KENNEDY

Racism. It has so thoroughly poisoned Americans of all colors that many of us can simply not see beyond it.

MARTHA QUINTANALES

Every person must have a concern for self, and feel a responsibility to discover one's mission in life. . . . Potential powers of creativity are within us, and we have a duty to work assiduously to discover these powers.

MARTIN LUTHER KING, JR.

While it is critical to understand the scope and magnitude of the crisis afflicting our nation's children, it is important not to become overwhelmed and paralyzed, nor to lose sight of the very human faces and lives represented by the numbers.

SHANNON DALY

If you have made mistakes . . . there is always another chance for you . . . you may have a fresh start any moment you choose, for this thing we call "failure" is not the falling down, but the staying down.

MARY PICKFORD

You don't get there *because*, you get there *in spite of.*

JANET COLLINS

There is little place in the political scheme of things for an independent, creative personality, for a fighter. Anyone who takes that role must pay a price.

SHIRLEY CHISHOLM

To love without role, without power plays, is revolution.

RITA MAE BROWN

17

If folks can learn to be racist, then they can learn to be antiracist. If being a sexist ain't genetic, then, dad gum, people can learn about gender equality.

JOHNNETTA BETSCH COLE

Ideas won't keep. Something must be done about them.

ALFRED NORTH WHITEHEAD

Think of ideas as a beat. To change a mind is to change the world.

JOAN KONNER

The health of a democratic society may be measured by the quality of functions performed by private citizens.

ALEXIS DE TOCQUEVILLE

Someday after mastering the winds, the waves, the tides and gravity, we shall harness for God the energies of love. And then for the second time in the history of the world, man will have discovered fire.

PIERRE TEILHARD DE CHARDIN

We have to improve life, not just for those who have the most skills and those who know how to manipulate the system. But also for and with those who often have so much to give but never get the opportunity.

DOROTHY HEIGHT

Our answer is the world's hope: it is to rely on youth. . . . This world demands the qualities of youth; not a time of life but a state of mind, a temper of the will, a quality of the imagination, a predominance of courage over timidity, or the appetite for adventure over the love of ease.

ROBERT F. KENNEDY

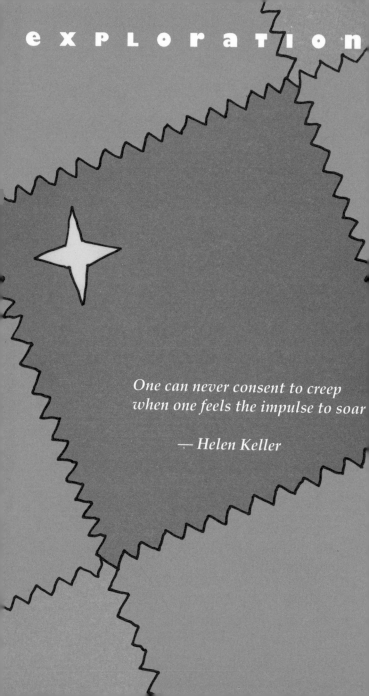

*One can never consent to creep
when one feels the impulse to soar*

— Helen Keller

Exploration

One can never consent to creep when
one feels the impulse to soar.
Helen Keller

The desk is a dangerous place from which
to watch the world.

JOHN LE CARRÉ

Love is a force. . . . It is not a result, it is a
cause. It is not a product; it produces. It is a
power, like money, or steam, or electricity. It
is valueless unless you can give something
else by means of it.

ANNE MORROW LINDBERGH

A university should be a place of light, of
liberty and of learning.

BENJAMIN DISRAELI

We must cultivate our garden.

VOLTAIRE

The best is the enemy of the good.

VOLTAIRE

The tough-minded respect difference. Their goal is a world made safe for differences.

RUTH FULTON BENEDICT

It requires something more than personal experience to gain a philosophy or point of view from any specific event. It is the quality of our response to the event and our capacity to enter into the lives of others that help us to make their lives and their experiences our own.

EMMA GOLDMAN

It just seems to me that as long as we are both here, it's pretty clear that the struggle is to share the planet, rather than to divide it.

ALICE WALKER

Definitions are limiting. Limitations are deadening. To limit oneself is a kind of suicide. To limit another is a kind of murder.

TOM ROBBINS

My definition of a free society is a society where it is safe to be unpopular.

ADLAI E. STEVENSON

If a man hasn't discovered something that he will die for, he isn't fit to live.

MARTIN LUTHER KING, JR.

So high as a tree aspires to grow, so high
will it find an atmosphere suited to it.

HENRY DAVID THOREAU

Heaven is living in your hopes, and Hell is
living in your fears.

TOM ROBBINS

And the trouble is, if you don't risk
anything, you risk even more.

ERICA JONG

Go ahead and fail. But fail with wit, fail with
grace, fail with style. . . . Embrace failure!
Seek it out. Learn to love it. That may be the
only way any of us will ever be free.

TOM ROBBINS

Your daring has to be backed up with a
willingness to lose that point. To make a
bigger point, you may have to lose one.

KATHERINE DUNHAM

Four things come not back—the spoken
word, the sped arrow, the past life, and the
neglected opportunity.

ARABIAN PROVERB

The fool wonders, the wise man asks.

BENJAMIN DISRAELI

People almost always do great things
without knowing how to do them, and are
quite surprised to have done them.

BERNARD DE FONTENELLE

When we can't dream any longer, we die.

EMMA GOLDMAN

A child educated only at school is an
uneducated child.

GEORGE SANTAYANA

The great difficulty in education is to get
experience out of ideas.

GEORGE SANTAYANA

You can't hold a man down without staying
down with him.

BOOKER T. WASHINGTON

Civilization is a race between education and catastrophe.

H. G. WELLS

A university does great things, but there is one thing it does not do; it does not intellectualize its neighborhood.

JOHN HENRY, CARDINAL NEWMAN

We have to dare to be ourselves, however frightening or strange that self may prove to be.

MAY SARTON

I like the dreams of the future better than the history of the past.

THOMAS JEFFERSON

The object of education is to prepare the young to educate themselves throughout their lives.

ROBERT MAYNARD HUTCHINS

Those who profess to favor freedom, and yet depreciate agitation, are men who want rain without thunder and lightning.

FREDERICK DOUGLASS

When choosing between two evils, I always like to try the one I've never tried before

MAE WEST

I am an idealist. I don't know where I'm going but I'm on my way.

CARL SANDBURG

The master's tools will never dismantle the master's house.

AUDRE LORDE

If a man does not keep pace with his companions, perhaps it is because he hears a different drummer. Let him step to the music which he hears, however measured or far away.

HENRY DAVID THOREAU

Life is either a daring adventure or nothing.

HELEN KELLER

If you don't know where you are going to, you will end up somewhere else.

LEWIS CARROLL,
Alice in Wonderland

Imagination is more important than
knowledge.

ALBERT EINSTEIN

Think wrongly, if you please, but in all cases
think for yourself.

DORIS LESSING

Human progress is neither automatic nor
inevitable . . . This is no time for apathy or
complacency. This is a time for vigorous
positive action.

MARTIN LUTHER KING, JR.

It is time for a new generation of leadership
to cope with new problems and new
opportunities. For there is a new world to
be won.

JOHN F. KENNEDY

Avoiding danger is no safer in the long run than outright exposure. The fearful are caught as often as the bold.

HELEN KELLER

I can't be found in myself; I discover myself in others. That much is clear. And I suspect that I also love and care for myself in others.

HUGH PRATHER

Indifference is the invincible giant of the world.

OUIDA

action

*Ain't nothin' to it
but to do it.*

— Maya Angelou

Action

Ain't nothin' to it but to do it.
Maya Angelou

From a little spark may burst a mighty
flame.

DANTE

He who considers too much will perform
little.

SCHILLER

Talents are best nurtured in solitude;
character is best formed in the stormy
billows of the world.

GOETHE

It is best for men, when they take counsel,
to be timorous, and imagine all possible
calamities, but when the time for action
comes, then to deal boldly.

HERODOTUS

The great pleasure in life is doing what
people say you cannot do.

WALTER BAGEHOT

Chance works for us when we are good
captains.

GEORGE MEREDITH

No choice is a choice too.

YIDDISH PROVERB

Conditions are never just right.

WILLIAM FEATHER

Courage is rightly esteemed the first of
human qualities because it is the quality
which guarantees all others.

WINSTON CHURCHILL

Leadership is action, not position.

DONALD H. MCGANNON

The great end of life is not knowledge but
action.

THOMAS HENRY HUXLEY

Courage is grace under pressure.

ERNEST HEMINGWAY

One man with courage makes a majority.

ANDREW JACKSON

Destiny is not a matter of chance, it is a
matter of choice; it is not a thing to be
waited for, it is a thing to be achieved.

WILLIAM JENNINGS BRYAN

I studied the lives of great men and famous
women, and I found that the men and
women who got to the top were those who
did the jobs they had in hand, with
everything they had of energy and
enthusiasm and hard work.

HARRY S. TRUMAN

A hero is no braver than an ordinary man,
but he is braver five minutes longer.

RALPH WALDO EMERSON

There is one thing stronger than all the
armies in the world: and that is an idea
whose time has come.

VICTOR HUGO

If you would be leader of men, you must
lead your own generation, not the next.

WOODROW WILSON

Lord, grant that I may always desire more
than I can accomplish.

MICHELANGELO

Remember, no one can make you feel
inferior without your consent.

ELEANOR ROOSEVELT

Raise less corn and more hell.

"MOTHER" LEASE

These are the times that try men's souls. The
summer soldier and the sunshine patriot
will, in this crisis, shrink from the service of
his country; but he that stands it *now*
deserves the love and thanks of man and
woman.

THOMAS PAINE

I hold it, that a little rebellion, now and then,
is a good thing, and as necessary in the
political world as storms in the physical.

THOMAS JEFFERSON

We have to face the fact that either all of us are going to die together or we are going to learn to live together and if we are to live together we have to talk.

ELEANOR ROOSEVELT

Direct action is not a substitute for work in the courts and the halls of government. . . . Indeed, direct action and legal action complement one another; when skillfully employed, each becomes more effective.

MARTIN LUTHER KING, JR.

Make yourself necessary to someone.

RALPH WALDO EMERSON

Great thoughts speak only to the thoughtful mind, but great actions speak to all mankind.

EMILY P. BISSELL

If you want to innovate, to change an enterprise or a society, it takes people willing to do what's not expected.

JEAN RIBOUD

No one has yet fully realized the wealth of sympathy, kindness and generosity hidden in the soul of a child. The effort of every true education should be to unlock that treasure . . .

EMMA GOLDMAN

For it isn't enough to talk about peace. One must believe in it. And it isn't enough to believe in it. One must work at it.

ELEANOR ROOSEVELT

The outrage of hunger amidst plenty will never be solved by "experts" somewhere. It will only be solved when people like you and me decide to act.

FRANCES MOORE LAPPÉ

There is no substitute for hard work.

THOMAS EDISON

Treat people as if they were what they
ought to be, and help them become what
they are capable of being.

GOETHE

We can do anything we want to do if we
stick to it long enough.

HELEN KELLER

Complacency is a far more dangerous
attitude than outrage.

NAOMI LITTLEBEAR

The prime function of a leader is to keep hope alive.

JOHN W. GARDNER

It is not enough to allow dissent. We must demand it.

ROBERT F. KENNEDY

Every great and commanding moment in the annals of the world is the triumph of some enthusiasm.

RALPH WALDO EMERSON

Giving kids clothes and food is one thing but it's much more important to teach them that other people besides themselves are important, and that the best thing they can do with their lives is to use them in the service of other people.

DOLORES HUERTA

Masterpieces are not single and solitary
births; they are the outcome of many years
of thinking in common, of thinking by the
body of the people, so that the experience of
the mass is behind the single voice.

VIRGINIA WOOLF

There is no such thing as making the
miracle happen spontaneously and on the
spot. You've got to work.

MARTINA ARROYO

We need love and creative imagination to
do constructive work.

PAULA OLLENDORF

Grab the broom of anger and drive off the
beast of fear.

ZORA NEALE HURSTON

reFLecTIon

*Nothing can bring you
peace but yourself.*

— *Ralph Waldo Emerson*

Reflection

Nothing can bring you peace but yourself.
Ralph Waldo Emerson

Five strokes of love for every stroke of
challenge.

GREG RICKS

You should always know when you're
shifting gears in life. You should leave your
era, it should never leave you.

LEONTYNE PRICE

In the depths of winter, I finally learned that
within me there lay an invincible summer.

ALBERT CAMUS

Work is love made visible.

KAHLIL GIBRAN

45

Perhaps, someday, even this distress will be a joy to recall.

VIRGIL

Though nothing can bring back the hour of splendor in the grass, or glory in the flower; we will grieve not, rather find strength in what remains behind.

WILLIAM WORDSWORTH

You will make all kinds of mistakes; but as long as you are generous and true, and also fierce, you cannot hurt the world or even seriously distress her. She was made to be wooed and won by youth.

WINSTON CHURCHILL

Study without reflection is a waste of time; reflection without study is dangerous.

CONFUCIUS

It is not enough to be busy; so are the ants.
The question is: What are we busy about?

HENRY DAVID THOREAU

Know Thyself.

SOCRATES

I will study and get ready and the
opportunity will come.

ABRAHAM LINCOLN

What I must do, is all that concerns me, not
what the people think . . . It is easy in the
world to live after the world's opinion; it is
easy in solitude to live after our own; but
the great man is he who in the midst of the
crowd keeps with perfect sweetness the
independence of solitude.

RALPH WALDO EMERSON

These three things—work, will, success—fill human existence. Will opens the door to success, both brilliant and happy. Work passes these doors, and at the end of the journey success comes in to crown one's efforts.

LOUIS PASTEUR

I shall allow no man to belittle my soul by making me hate him.

BOOKER T. WASHINGTON

A cynical young person is almost the saddest sight to see because it means that he or she has gone from knowing nothing to believing in nothing.

MAYA ANGELOU

An individual has not started living until he can rise above the narrow confines of his individualistic concerns to the broader concerns of all humanity.

MARTIN LUTHER KING, JR.

The humblest citizen of all the land, when clad in the armor of a righteous cause, is stronger than all the hosts of Error.

WILLIAM JENNINGS BRYAN

I'm not an American hero. I'm a person that loves children.

MOTHER HALE

Compassion and nonviolence help us to see the enemy's point of view, to hear his questions, to know his assessment of ourselves. For from his view we may indeed see the basic weaknesses of our own condition, and if we are mature, we may learn and grow and profit from the wisdom of the brothers who are called the opposition.

MARTIN LUTHER KING, JR.

The gem cannot be polished without friction, nor man perfected without trials.

CONFUCIUS

Everything that is done in the world is done by hope. No husbandman would sow one grain of corn if he hoped not it would grow up and become seed; no bachelor would marry a wife if he hoped not to have children; no merchant or tradesman would set himself to work if he did not hope to reap benefit thereby.

MARTIN LUTHER

We don't see things as they are, we see things as we are.

ANAÏS NIN

No type of injustice is more glaring than that of the hypocrite who, in the very instant of being most false, makes the pretense of appearing virtuous.

CICERO

When in doubt, tell the truth.

MARK TWAIN

There is nothing permanent except change.

HERACLITUS

Where is there dignity unless there is
honesty?

CICERO

Diplomacy is the art of letting someone else
have your way.

DANIELE VARE

Emotion is the chief source of all becoming
conscious. There can be no transforming of
darkness into light and of apathy into
movement without emotion.

ERIC JUNG

Eternity is not something that begins after you are dead. It is going on all the time. We are in it now.

CHARLOTTE PERKINS GILMAN

Praise to a human being represents what sunlight, water, and soil are to a plant—the climate in which one grows best.

EARL NIGHTINGALE

There is a spirit and a need and a man at the beginning of every great human advance. Each of these must be right for that particular moment of history, or nothing happens.

CORETTA SCOTT KING

The shoe that fits one person pinches another; there is no recipe for living that suits all cases. Each of us carries his own life-form . . .

ERIC JUNG

To keep our faces toward change and behave like free spirits in the presence of fate is strength undefeatable.

HELEN KELLER

If there is anything that we wish to change in the child, we should first examine to see whether it is not something that had better be changed in ourselves.

ERIC JUNG

I had reasoned this out in my mind, there was two things I had a right to, liberty and death. If I could not have one, I would have the other, for no man should take me alive.

HARRIET TUBMAN

Solitude is a silent storm that breaks down all our dead branches. Yet it sends our living roots deeper into the living heart of the living earth.

KAHLIL GIBRAN

I respect my work for the reason that no
one else does.

YURI KAGEYAMA

Getting ahead in a difficult profession
requires avid faith in yourself. You must be
able to sustain yourself against staggering
blows and unfair reversals. There is no code
of conduct to help beginners. That is why
some people with mediocre talent, but with
great inner drive, go much further than
people with vastly superior talent.

SOPHIA LOREN

The place of the dance is within the heart.

TOM ROBBINS

I am what I am. Take it or leave me alone.

ROSARIO MORALES

Live to learn and you will learn to live.

PORTUGUESE PROVERB

Don't compromise yourself. You are all
you've got.

JANIS JOPLIN

One of the oldest human needs is having
someone to wonder where you are when
you don't come home at night.

MARGARET MEAD

when words & manners leave you no space
for yrself/make a poem/very
personal/very clear/& yr obstructions will
join you or disappear/

NTOZAKE SHANGE

If you're going to hold someone down
you're going to have to hold onto the other
end of the chain. You are confined by your
own repression.

TONI MORRISON

My mission on earth is to recognize the
void—inside and outside of me—and fill it.

RABBI MENAHEM

CELEBRATION

We ourselves must be full of life if we are going to make life fuller for others.

— *David Sawyer*

Celebration

We ourselves must be full of life if we are going to make life fuller for others.
David Sawyer

Being on a tightrope is living, everything else is just waiting.

KARL WALLENDA

We can do no great things—only small things with great love.

MOTHER TERESA

To be successful, the first thing to do is fall in love with your work.

SISTER MARY LAURETTA

Be good to yourself,
Be excellent to others and
Do everything with love.

JOHN WOLF

It is not the critic who counts, not the man who points out how the strong man stumbled, or where the doer of deeds could have done them better.

The credit belongs to the man who is actually in the arena; whose face is marred by dust and sweat and blood; who strives valiantly; who errs and comes short again and again; who knows the great enthusiasms, the great devotions, and spends himself in a worthy cause; who, at best, knows in the end the triumph of high achievement; and who, at the worst, if he fails, at least fails while daring greatly, so that his place shall never be with those cold and timid souls who know neither victory nor defeat.

THEODORE ROOSEVELT

In the struggle for justice, the only reward is the opportunity to be in the struggle. You can't expect that you're going to have it tomorrow. You just have to keep working on it.

FREDERICK DOUGLASS

The Eskimo has fifty-two names for snow
because it is important to them; there ought
to be as many for love.

MARGARET ATWOOD

Every now and then I think about my own
death, and I think about my own funeral.
. . . if you get someone to deliver the
eulogy, tell them not to talk too long. Tell
them not to mention that I have a Nobel
Peace Prize. . . . Tell them not to mention
that I have three or four hundred other
awards. . . . I'd like for somebody to say that
day that Martin Luther King, Jr. tried to love
somebody, . . .

Say that I was a drum major for justice.
Say that I was a drum major for peace. That
I was a drum major for righteousness. . . . I
won't have any money to leave behind. I
won't have the fine and luxurious things of
life to leave behind. But I just want to leave
a committed life behind.

MARTIN LUTHER KING, JR.

You will do foolish things, but do them with enthusiasm.

COLETTE

If you can walk you can dance. If you can talk you can sing.

ZIMBABWE SAYING

If only I could so live and so serve the world that after me there should never again be birds in cages . . .

ISAK DINESEN

While there's life, there's hope.

CICERO

At the end of this century, which has seen so much suffering and misery, today's young generation has a chance like hardly any preceding one: the chance of a full life in peace and freedom. And the young generation has every reason to be optimistic in its pursuit of happiness.

HELMUT KOHL

Everybody has their ups and downs so I decided to have mine between good and great.

DANIEL HOOGTERP

No man or woman, even of the humblest sort, can really be strong, gentle, pure and good without the world being better for it; without somebody being helped and comforted by the very existence of that goodness.

PHILLIPS BROOKS

Love grows by service.

CHARLOTTE PERKINS GILMAN

Life must be lived moment by moment.
Each moment carries a message, a lesson for
us.

DR. DAVID K. REYNOLDS

To live is so startling it leaves little time for
anything else.

EMILY DICKINSON

The final test of a leader is that he leaves
behind him in other men the conviction and
the will to carry on. . . . The genius of a good
leader is to leave behind him a situation
which common sense, without the grace of
genius, can deal with successfully.

WALTER LIPPMANN

Follow what you love! . . . Don't deign to ask what "they" are looking for out there. Ask what you have inside. Follow not your interests, which change, but what you are and what you love, which will and should not change.

GEORGIE ANNE GEYER

The most visible creators I know of are those artists whose medium is life itself. The ones who express the inexpressible—without brush, hammer, clay or guitar. They neither paint nor sculpt—their medium is being. Whatever their presence touches has increased life. They see and don't have to draw. They are the artists of being alive.

J. STONE

Love, the magician, knows this little trick whereby two people walk in different directions yet always remain side by side.

HUGH PRATHER

Contributors

David Battey
A. Denise Beal
John Beilenson
Rebecca Breuer
Alex Byrd
Kathy Connelly
Shannon Daley
Bobby Hackett
Bill Hoogterp
Rich James
Jennifer Kurkoski
Roger Landrum
Tanya Lieberman
Genevieve Lynch
Borden Mace
Amy Mast
David McDaniels
Louisa Meacham
Carolyn Mecker
Catherine Milton
Roger Nozaki
Bruce Payne
Lara Pratt
Greg Ricks
Ullyses Sanchez
Todd Savage
David Sawyer
Julia Scatliff
Amy Schoenblum
Frank Slobig
April Smith
Mary Vase
John Wallace
Laina Warsavage
Jamie Watson
K. P. Weseloh
Katie Wolf
Maura C. Wolf
Lee Wood
Karen Young

All the students and individuals who, in a speech or a letter, or through their work, have given us a reason and inspiration to continue our work.